Introducing Religions

Christianity

Sue Penney

www.heinemann.co.uk/library
Visit our website to find out more information about Heinemann Library books.

To order:
☎ Phone 44 (0) 1865 888066
📄 Send a fax to 44 (0) 1865 314091
💻 Visit the Heinemann Bookshop at www.heinemann.co.uk/library to browse our catalogue and order online.

First published in Great Britain by Heinemann Library, Halley Court, Jordan Hill, Oxford OX2 8EJ, part of Harcourt Education.
Heinemann is a registered trademark of Harcourt Education Ltd.

Editorial: Clare Lewis
Design: Jo Hinton-Malivoire and Q2A Creative
Illustrations: Gecko Limited
Picture Research: Erica Newbury
Production: Helen McCreath

Printed and bound in China by WKT.

10 digit ISBN 0 431 06653 1
13 digit ISBN 978 0 431 06653 0
10 09 08 07 06
10 9 8 7 6 5 4 3 2 1

British Library Cataloguing in Publication Data
Penney, Sue
Christianity (Introducing Religions – 2nd edition)
200
A full catalogue record for this book is available from the British Library.

Acknowledgements
The publishers would like to thank the following for permission to reproduce photographs:
The Ancient Art and Architecture Collection p. 37; Andes Press Agency pp. 9, 11 (right), 18 (both), 22, 23 (left); The Bridgeman Art Library pp. 25, 26; Palll Bryans p. 16 (right); Cambridge Evening News p. 46 (top); Circa Photo Library p. 48; C M Dixon p. 35; Corbis pp. 10, 21, 38; Keith Ellis pp. 23 (right), 44; Mary Evans Picture Library p. 36; Glasgow Museums: the St Mungo Museum of Religious Life and Art p. 29; Sally and Richard Greenhill p. 45, 46 (below); Sonia Halliday Photographs pp. 19, 27, 32, 33; Robert Harding Picture Library p. 11 (left); J Allan Cash Photo Library pp. 8, 17, 42, 49; Philip Parkhouse p. 40; Ann and Bury Peerless p. 41; Frank Spooner Pictures p. 13; Zefa pp. 12, 15, 16 (left), 43.

The photograph on the previous page is reproduced by permission of Alamy/Robert Harding World Imagery.

Cover photograph of Orthodox Christian clergy during the Ethiopian celebration of Epiphany, reproduced with permission of Corbis/Wendy Stone.

The publishers would like to thank Jo Turkas for her assistance in the preparation of this book.

Every effort has been made to contact copyright holders of any material reproduced in this book. Any omissions will be rectified in subsequent printings if notice is given to the publishers.

The paper used to print this book comes from sustainable resources.

Contents

Words that are printed in bold, **like this**, are explained in the glossary on page 50.

MAP: where the main religions began

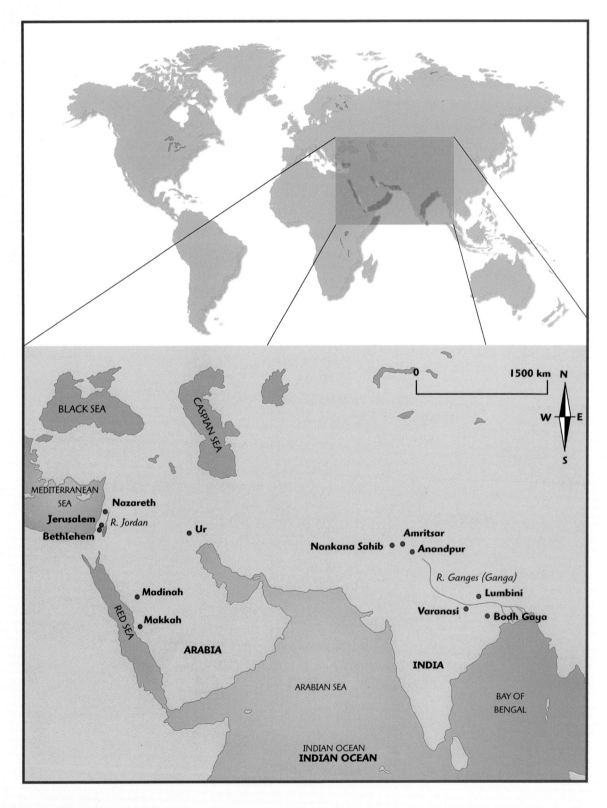

TIMECHART: when the main religions began

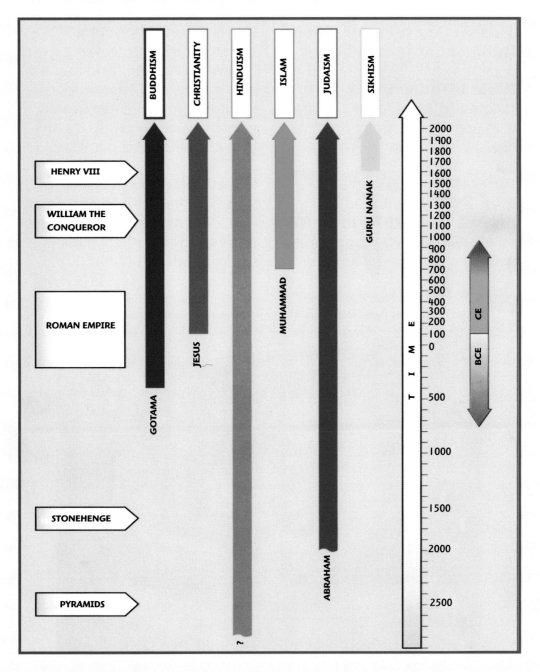

Note about dating systems *In this book dates are not called BC and AD, which is the Christian dating system. The letters BCE and CE are used instead. BCE stands for "Before the Common Era" and CE stands for "Common Era". BCE and CE can be used by people of all religions, Christians too. The year numbers are not changed.*

Introducing Christianity

This section tells you something about who Christians are.

What is Christianity?

Christianity is the religion of people who are Christians. Christians believe in God and follow the teachings of Jesus. They believe that Jesus was God's son.

What do Christians believe about God?

Christians usually talk about God as "he", but they do not believe he is a man. They believe that God is a **spirit**. This means he does not have a body like a person or an animal does.

Christians believe that God was never born and will never die. God sees and knows everything. God made all things, and he loves everything he made. Christians say that people can know what God is like because of the life of Jesus.

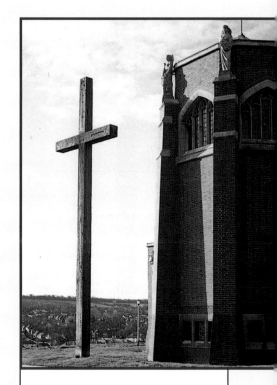

The cross is a sign used by Christians.

What do Christians believe about Jesus?

Jesus was a man who lived on earth about 2,000 years ago. Christians call him Jesus **Christ**.

The name "Christian" comes from the word "Christ". It was not Jesus's last name. It means "someone God has chosen". Using this name shows that Christians believe Jesus was special. They believe that he was closer to God than anyone else who has ever lived.

The fish symbol is on this altar cover.

Jesus died when he was nailed to a wooden cross (see pages 28-29). Christians believe that Jesus's death was very important.

They also believe that he came back from the dead, and is still alive. They do not think that he still has a body like ours.

Jesus's coming back to life is called the **Resurrection**. Believing in the Resurrection is very important for Christians. They believe it shows there is life after death.

Signs that Christians use

Most religions use signs to show what they believe. Christians often use the sign of a cross. This is because Jesus died on a cross. Sometimes they use the sign of a fish. One reason for this is because some of the first Christians were fishermen.

God be in my head

This poem was written by Christians hundreds of years ago. It shows that Christians believe being close to God is important.

God be in my head
  and in my understanding;
God be in my eyes
  and in my looking;
God be in my mouth
  and in my speaking;
God be in my heart
  and in my thinking;
God be at mine end
  and at my departing.

The Roman Catholic Church

This section tells you about one of the largest groups of Christians in the world.

What is a church?
The word **church** can be used in two ways. It can mean the building where Christians meet together to **worship**. Worship includes things such as praying (talking to God), singing, and talking about God. The word **Church** can also mean a group of Christians who worship in the same way, such as the Roman Catholic Church or the Methodist Church. When it is used in this way, Church usually has a capital C.

The Roman Catholic Church
The Roman Catholic Church makes up one of the largest groups of Christians. About half of all Christians are Roman Catholics.

The Pope
Roman Catholics believe that the most important person in the Church is the **Pope**. "Pope" comes from a word that means father, so the Pope is like a father to the Church.

Roman Catholics believe that the Pope is very close to God. When a Pope dies, a new Pope is chosen by the most senior men in the Church.

Mary the mother of Jesus
Roman Catholics believe that Mary was special because she was the mother of Jesus. They call her "Our Lady", and they often pray to her. A popular prayer begins "Hail Mary full of grace".

Saints
Roman Catholics often pray to **saints**. Saints are special people who were very close to God when they were alive. (There is more about saints on pages 36–37.)

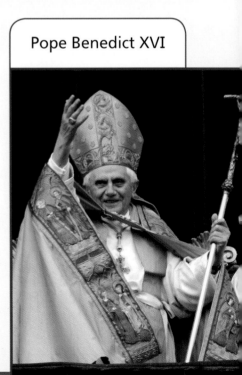
Pope Benedict XVI

A statue of Mary and Jesus

Rosary beads help people pray.

Priests

Only men can become Roman Catholic **priests**. They are not allowed to marry, so they have more time to spend on their work. They are trained to lead worship and help people. A priest also hears **confessions**, when people tell him all the wrong things they have done, and say they are sorry.

Why are there different Churches?

There are millions of Christians all over the world. Not all of them believe exactly the same things. They all believe in God, and that Jesus was the Son of God. Other beliefs are more important to some people than to others. For example, people who are Roman Catholics believe that Mary the mother of Jesus was very important.

Other Christians do not agree with this. People who think in the same way often want to worship together. These groups are called Churches. There are thousands of different Churches all over the world. Some have millions of members while others have only a few. Each Church worships in its own way.

The Orthodox Churches

This section tells you about the Orthodox Churches.

The Orthodox **Churches** are one of the oldest parts of Christianity.

There are some differences between what Orthodox Christians believe and what other Christians believe. These differences are because of disagreements that happened between church leaders nearly 1,000 years ago. They disagreed about what parts of their beliefs were most important. The Orthodox Churches say that their beliefs are most like the beliefs of the first Christians.

Where do Orthodox Christians live?
There are many different Orthodox Churches. Most Orthodox Christians live in Russia and Greece. They belong to the Russian and Greek Orthodox Churches.

Many thousands live in other parts of the world, too. There are about 500,000 Orthodox Christians living in the UK.

Inside an Orthodox church
Orthodox churches are usually beautifully decorated. They are sometimes painted in gold. The people want the church to look beautiful to show that it is a very special place. They want it to show how much they love God.

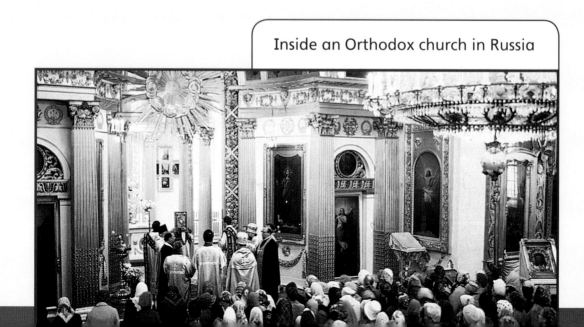

Inside an Orthodox church in Russia

Icons are painted very carefully.

Some Orthodox churches do not have seats. The people stand to **worship**. Orthodox churches are divided in two by a special screen. The screen hides the **altar** from the rest of the church. The altar is a special table (see page 18). The screen has doors in it. Only the priests can go through the doors, but they are open when people are worshipping. This is to show that there is a way to God.

Icons

Some of the most important things in an Orthodox church are special pictures called **icons**. Icons are beautifully painted by hand. They show Jesus or Mary, or sometimes one of the saints. When Orthodox Christians go into the church, they light a candle in front of one of the icons and kiss the icon. The icons help them worship God.

Candles

Many Churches use candles in worship. For Roman Catholics and Orthodox Christians they are very important. Years ago, candles were needed to light the church when it was dark. Today, they are not needed in the same way, but they do help to make the church beautiful.

The main reason for using candles is that they are signs. They help to remind people of Jesus, because one of the names Christians use for Jesus is the Light of the World. Some people say that the reason there are two candles on the altar in some churches is to remind people that Jesus was both God and man. Special candles are used at Advent (see page 40) and at Easter (see pages 42–43).

The Protestant Churches

This section tells you about some Protestant Churches.

There are lots of different Protestant **Churches** all over the world. They are called Protestant because they began when people protested about things they thought were wrong with the Roman Catholic Church in the 16th century. Some Protestant Churches have millions of members, while others have far fewer. They are all Christians, but they **worship** in different ways.

The Anglican Church

The Anglican Church is the largest Church in the UK. Many countries have their own branch of the Anglican Church. In England, it is the Church of England. In Scotland, it is called the Episcopal Church. In Wales, it is called the Church in Wales. In Ireland, it is the Church of Ireland. In the United States, it is the Episcopal Church of the USA.

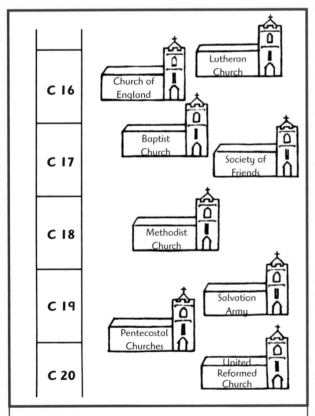

This shows when some Churches began. (C = Century CE).

In other countries, the Anglican Church often takes the name of the country. For example, the Anglican Church of Australia and the Anglican Church of Canada.

Anglicans call the local area a **parish**, so **churches** are often called parish churches. They are usually named after a saint. For example, "the parish church of St Paul".

The people who lead worship are often called **vicars**. Most vicars are men, but women can also become vicars. Senior vicars are called **bishops**. The most important bishop in the Church of England is called the Archbishop of Canterbury.

A Protestant church service

Other Churches

There are many other Protestant Churches. Each Church has beliefs which other Churches do not share or do not think are so important. In the UK, after the Anglican Church, the Churches with most members are the Presbyterian Churches and the Methodist Church. Each Church has its own way of worship.

Other groups

There are many other groups of Christians in the world. This book does not have room to mention them all.

Most groups have teachings which are special to their own people. Some groups have teachings which are not accepted by the main Churches.

Christian beliefs about God

All the first Christians had been brought up as Jews. They believed that there was only one God. But they also believed that Jesus was God. How could Jesus have been a man alive on earth, and still be God?

The explanation is called the Trinity. This is the belief that God can be seen in three ways – God the Father, God the Son, and God the **Holy Spirit**. Christians say that God the Father is a spirit who never changes. When Jesus was alive on earth he was completely man but also completely God. God the Holy Spirit is the way that God's power can be seen working in the world.

Church buildings: outside

This section tells you about the places where Christians meet to worship.

Church buildings can be very large or very small. Some are hundreds of years old, some are new. They may have lots of decoration, or none. Churches can even be in ordinary houses.

Cathedrals

Some churches are more important than others. The most important Roman Catholic, Orthodox, and Anglican churches are called **cathedrals**.

Many cathedrals are very old. They are often built in stone, with strong wooden doors. Decorations may be carved into the stone.

The shape of a church

Many churches and cathedrals are built in the shape of a cross, because Jesus died on a cross. Orthodox churches are often square. Some modern churches are round, so that all the people **worshipping** can see clearly.

An Orthodox church in Birmingham

The Roman Catholic cathedral in Liverpool

Many churches have part of the building higher than the rest. If this is square it is called a tower. If it is pointed it is called a **spire**. Churches often have a clock and bells, too. A long time ago, people did not have clocks of their own. The church clock and bells told them when it was time to go to church. Today, people still ring the bells when it is time for worship. They also ring the bells at special times such as weddings and funerals.

The way a church is built often tells you a lot about its history. For example, a church with thick stone walls and small windows is usually very old. A church with pointed windows and more decorations is more recent.

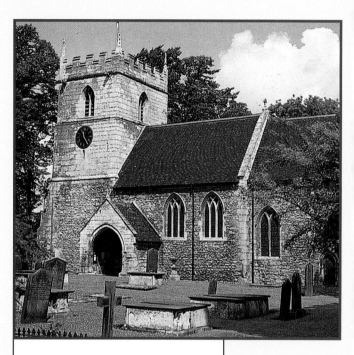

A typical parish church

Churchyards

Many churches have an area of land around them called the churchyard. This often has many graves in it, where the bodies of people who have died are buried. Some bodies are still buried there today, but many churchyards are now full, and bodies are buried in a cemetery instead.

Yew trees are often found in churchyards. There are many reasons for this. A yew tree grows very thick and strong, and can live for hundreds of years. It can help to protect the church from storms. Yew berries are poisonous, so farmers kept their animals away from them. Long ago, people did not think it was right for animals to eat the grass in churchyards.

Church buildings: inside

This section tells you about some of the things you may find inside a church.

All **churches** are different. Some have lots of decorations inside, some are very plain. Usually, Orthodox and Roman Catholic churches have the most decorations.

Not all churches have the same things inside. Modern churches may be especially different.

Altar

The **altar** is the most important part of most churches. It is a special table made of wood or stone. In some churches, it is called the Communion table.

It is used in the service called **Holy Communion**, also called the **Eucharist**. This is the most important part of **worship** for most Christians. (The Eucharist is described on pages 22–23.)

Lectern

Most churches have a special reading desk called a lectern. It is often made of brass and in the shape of an eagle. A Bible is kept on it. The Bible is the Christians' holy book.

Pulpit

A pulpit is usually at the front of the church. It is usually made of wood or stone.

The person giving the special talk which is part of the worship climbs the steps to get into the pulpit. Then everyone in the church can see him or her easily.

Inside a Roman Catholic church

A font made of carved stone

Font

A font is a special basin for water. The water is used for **baptisms**. Baptism is a special service when people join the Church. Fonts are made of wood or stone. They often have decorations carved on them.

Stained glass windows

Many churches have windows made with glass in bright colours. This is called stained glass. Sometimes the glass just makes a pattern. Sometimes it has pictures which tell a story. Long ago, many people could not read or write, so the pictures in the windows helped them to understand the stories they heard in church.

Banners

Many churches are decorated with banners. These may be very old, or they may have been made by someone who worships at the church. They are often beautifully embroidered.

Usually at least one banner includes the name of the church. This is carried in church processions – for example, at Pentecost (see page 42). It may have a picture of the church, or of the saint that the church is named after. Other banners may have the name of groups at the church – for example, Sunday School, or Cubs and Brownies.

A modern stained glass window

Christian worship

This section tells you about how Christians worship.

Christians think **worshipping** God is important. Worship means thinking about God and praising God. Christians can worship God anywhere. They do not have to be in a special place or with anyone else. Most Christians do worship with other people, because they think it is important to meet in a group.

A meeting for worship is often called a **service**. This is usually held on a Sunday. Christians believe that Sunday is the day when Jesus rose from the dead. Services in different **Churches** are not the same. This section tells you about things that happen in many services.

Prayers

Prayer means talking and listening to God. Christians believe God cares about the world like a father who loves his children. Praying is important. Some prayers tell God how much the people love him. Some say sorry for things they have done wrong and some ask God for help.

Christians believe that God listens and can answer prayers. An important prayer is called the **Lord's Prayer** (see opposite). Christians believe Jesus taught it to his friends and followers.

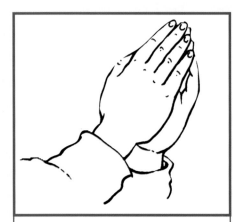

Christians often put their hands together when they pray.

Music

Most services include special songs called **hymns**. Christians sing hymns as part of worship. In most churches, there is an organ or a piano. Some churches use a band or guitars to help the people sing.

Bible readings

Most services have readings from the Bible. Christians believe that reading the Bible is important. Reading about Jesus helps Christians to learn about how they should live.

A Society of Friends meeting

Sermon

A sermon is a special talk. It is usually given from the pulpit by the **vicar**, **priest**, or someone else who is important in the Church. Sermons usually explain some of Jesus's teaching, and other passages from the Bible, and tell the people how to live as Christians.

Different ways of worship

Different churches worship in different ways. A **meeting** of the Society of Friends will sit in silence until someone feels God has chosen them to speak. The Salvation Army often hold services out of doors so people who would not come to church may still hear about Jesus. Some groups sing and dance as part of their worship.

These differences mean that all Christians can worship in a way that they feel is right for them.

The Lord's Prayer
Our Father in heaven
hallowed be your name,
your kingdom come,
your will be done,
on earth as in heaven.
Give us today our daily bread.
Forgive us our sins
as we forgive those who sin
against us.
Lead us not into temptation
but deliver us from evil.
For the kingdom, the power,
and the glory are yours
now and for ever.
Amen.

The Eucharist

This section tells you about an important Christian service.

The **Eucharist** is a very special **service** for most Christians. It has different names in different **Churches**. It is often called **Holy Communion**.

A Roman Catholic Mass

Holy Communion is the service where Christians eat a small piece of bread and drink a little wine. They believe that this bread and wine are important, because of the prayers that are said. The prayers makes ordinary bread and wine into something special.

Christians also believe they are doing what Jesus taught, because he told his friends "Do this to remember me". Taking part in a Eucharist service means that Christians can share something special. It helps them to feel closer to God.

The bread

In most Churches the bread is ordinary bread which has had special prayers said over it. Some Churches use a round wafer instead.

The **priest** or **vicar** gives some bread or a wafer to the people. He or she may say "The body of **Christ**". The people say "**Amen**". Amen is a word often used in prayers. It means "So be it". It is like saying "I agree".

The wine

The wine used for Holy Communion is often made so that it contains no alcohol. For the same reason, in some Churches red fruit juice is used instead of wine.

Sometimes it is in one large cup. Sometimes each person has a small glass. The priest or vicar gives the wine to the people. He or she may say "The blood of Christ". The people say "Amen".

In Orthodox Churches, the service is a little different. The priest gives the bread and wine together to the people on a spoon.

Orthodox Christians receive Communion from a spoon.

The Peace

In some Holy Communion services, the people shake hands or hug each other. They say "Peace be with you". This means that they are asking God to look after the person.

Holy Communion services end with prayers that thank God that the people have been able to worship him in this way.

Communion in a **parish** church

The Last Supper

Holy Communion reminds Christians of the last meal Jesus ate with his friends. This meal is called the Last Supper. Jesus took some bread and a cup of wine. He told his friends that the bread was like his body. The wine was like his blood. The bread was going to be broken and the wine was going to be poured. He said this to tell them that he was going to die. Jesus gave the bread and wine to his friends.

Christians believe Jesus's death was very important. It means people can reach God. Sharing the bread and wine in the Holy Communion service means Christians can join with Jesus in a special way.

The Bible

This section tells you about the Bible. The Bible is the Christians' holy book.

The Bible library
The Bible is called a book, but really it is 66 books that have been put together. The books can be divided into two parts. The first part is called the Old **Testament**. The second part is called the New Testament.

The Old Testament
The Old Testament comes from the holy books of Judaism. Judaism is one of the oldest world religions. Jesus was a Jew, and so were his friends. The Old Testament includes many different sorts of books. There are history books, story books, and poems. They show what the Jews learned about God.

Christians believe that the New Testament "finishes" the Old Testament. Jews do not agree. They believe that the Old Testament is complete in itself.

The New Testament
The first four books of the New Testament are called **Gospels**. The word comes from an old word which means "good news". The Gospels contain stories about Jesus. They are not a complete story of his life.

The men who wrote the Gospels wanted to show why they thought Jesus was special. They wrote about things he did and things he taught. A few stories are in all the Gospels, but most are in only one or two. Each writer chose the things he thought were most important.

The books that make up the Bible

A decorated capital letter in a handwritten Bible

The rest of the New Testament contains stories about the first Christians. It also contains letters written by some important early Christians.

How is the Bible used?

Christians believe that the Bible is the most important book that has ever been written. It helps them to understand what God is like, and it teaches them what is right and wrong.

Parts of the Bible are read at most **services** in **church**. Many Christians also read it carefully on their own at home, or together in small groups. They believe that knowing what the Bible teaches is an important part of their religion.

Handwritten Bibles

Before people knew how to print books with machines, the only copies of the Bible were written by hand. For hundreds of years, they were copied out by **monks** (see page 38).

The monks thought that the Bible was the most important book in the world, and they wanted to make their copies look beautiful. They decorated the writing with drawings. Sometimes these drawings were just pictures. More often, the drawings were made around capital letters. They were painted with coloured inks to make them look even more beautiful. Many of these Bibles can still be seen today.

The birth of Jesus

This section tells you about the birth of Jesus.

Jesus lived in the first century CE in the country called Palestine. Today we call it Israel. When Jesus was alive, Palestine was ruled by the Romans.

How do we know about Jesus?
Most of what we know about Jesus is written down in the **Gospels**. The Gospels are the first four books of the New **Testament** (see page 24). They were written by men who knew Jesus, or had talked to people who were his friends.

Jesus's name is also included in records written by the Romans.

What do we know about Jesus?
The men who wrote the Gospels were not trying to write a complete story of Jesus's life. Each of the Gospels includes small pieces of information.

If stories from the four Gospels are put together, we can find out more. Matthew's Gospel and Luke's Gospel tell of his birth.

The River Jordan was in Palestine.

Jesus's birth
Jesus's mother was called Mary. An **angel** told her she was going to have a baby, and she must call him Jesus. When it was almost time for the birth, the Romans ordered that everyone in the country had to be counted. They had to go back to where their family came from, to be counted there.

Mary and her husband Joseph had to go to the town of Bethlehem. While they were there, Jesus was born. The king of Palestine was called Herod. He heard about the new baby, and he was frightened.

A very old stained glass window showing the escape to Egypt

He thought the baby might be so special that he would take over as king when he grew up. To make sure this could not happen, King Herod ordered that all baby boys in Bethlehem should be killed. Mary and Joseph were warned about this in a dream. They escaped to the country called Egypt, and lived there for many years. They did not return to Palestine until after King Herod had died.

The childhood of Jesus

Not much is known about when Jesus was a child. Luke's Gospel says that when he was 12 years old Jesus went to Jerusalem with Mary and Joseph for the festival of the Passover.

When it was time to go home, Jesus was missing. Mary and Joseph found him in the **Temple**, the most important building in the Jewish religion. Mary asked Jesus if he had not realized they were worried. Jesus replied, "Didn't you know I would be in my father's house?"

Differences in the Gospels

Imagine going somewhere with a group of your friends. When you get back, you all tell another friend about the trip. None of you would say exactly the same things. The important bits would be the same, but the details would be different. Some people would remember one thing, some another. This is true for the Gospels, too.

The four Gospels were written by different people. Some of the writers may have known Jesus themselves. They had all talked to people who were Jesus's friends. Different people remembered different things about what Jesus had said and done. This is why the four Gospels are not exactly the same.

Jesus dies and rises again

This section tells you about Jesus's death and resurrection.

Jesus began teaching when he was about 30 years old. For about three years, he went from place to place teaching people. Friends went with him. Jesus's special friends are called his **disciples**. His three closest disciples were Peter, James, and John.

Ordinary people liked listening to Jesus. But the people who were in charge of the country of Palestine did not like some of the things that Jesus said. They were afraid what he said might turn the people against them. They decided they had to get rid of Jesus. They began to look for a chance to send soldiers to arrest him. They were afraid to arrest him when there were crowds of people around.

A painting showing the crucifixion of Jesus

Jesus is arrested
Jesus went to Jerusalem, which was the capital of Palestine. It was the time of a festival. Jesus shared a special meal with his disciples. This meal is called the **Last Supper** (see page 23).

Then they all went to a quiet garden. There were no crowds who might fight for Jesus. Soldiers came and arrested him. The Roman **Governor**, a man called Pontius Pilate, ordered that Jesus should be killed.

Jesus's death
Soldiers **crucified** Jesus. This means they nailed him to a cross made of wood. It was a very cruel way to kill people. After Jesus died, his friends took his body down from the cross. They put the body in a cave and rolled a rock across the entrance.

The body had gone!

This was what usually happened in those days when people died. Everyone thought that this was the end of Jesus.

Rising from the dead

The **Gospels** say that two days later, early on the Sunday morning, friends went to visit the grave. When they got to the cave, the stone had been moved.

The body had gone! Two men wearing shining white clothes told them that Jesus had risen from the dead! Christians believe that Jesus's rising from the dead is important. They call it the **Resurrection**. They believe it means that people who follow Jesus do not need to be afraid of death.

Jesus's last week

On *Palm Sunday* Jesus rode into Jerusalem on a donkey. The people were joyful and waved palm tree branches. On *Monday, Tuesday,* and *Wednesday* he taught people in Jerusalem. On *Maundy Thursday* he ate the Last Supper with his disciples. Later that night he was arrested.

On *Good Friday* morning Pontius Pilate ordered that Jesus should be killed. At midday he was crucified, and he died in the afternoon. His body was buried. On *Saturday*, his body was in the cave. On *Sunday* morning, disciples went to the cave. The body had gone. The Gospels say that later that day and in the next few weeks, his disciples saw him again many times.

Stories Jesus told

This section tells you about two of the stories that Jesus told.

When he was teaching, Jesus often told stories. Stories are interesting to listen to. They can make people think about the way they live. They can teach people lessons, too. Jesus's stories often had a meaning. A story with a meaning is called a **parable**.

One day Jesus was teaching about the right way to live. He wanted to show the people that they should care for anyone who needed their help. So he told them this story. You can find it in the Bible in Luke's **Gospel**, chapter 10 verses 25–37.

The parable of the good Samaritan

A Jewish man was walking from the city of Jerusalem to the town of Jericho. It was a lonely road, and he was attacked by robbers. They left him half-dead.

A man came by on his way to Jerusalem. Then another man walked past. They were both important people. They could have helped the man who was hurt. But they only wanted to look after themselves, and they walked on.

Then a Samaritan came past. He stopped and helped the man. He took him to an inn, and even paid for him to be looked after until he was better.

To understand this story, you need to know that in those days, Samaritans and Jews hated each other. The crowd who were listening would not have expected a Samaritan to help a Jew who had been attacked. The lesson of the story was clear to them. You should help anyone who needs it. It does not matter if it is someone you do not like, or someone you do not know.

The parable of the good Samaritan

The parable of the sower
(Mark's Gospel, chapter 4 verses 3–20)

A farmer went out to sow some seed. In those days, seed was sown by hand. As the farmer threw the seed, some of it fell in the wrong place. Some fell on the path and birds ate it. Some fell on ground where there was not much soil. It could not grow, and it died.

Some fell in weeds. It tried to grow, but there were too many weeds.

Some seed fell on good ground. It grew well, and gave a good crop.

Jesus said that the seed was like his teaching. Some people took no notice, but other people listened, and the teaching helped them live better lives.

The parable of the sower

Finding a story in the Bible
All the books in the Bible have names – for example, Mark's Gospel. Each book is split into smaller parts called chapters. Each chapter is split into smaller parts called verses. Each chapter and each verse has a number. This can be written as, for example, Mark 4: 20. The first number is the chapter, the second is the verse. These numbers stay the same in all Bibles. So you can always find a particular story if you know the name of the book, the chapter, and the verse.

Miracles Jesus worked

This section tells you about two of Jesus's miracles.

What is a miracle?

A **miracle** is something which happens but cannot be explained. It shows a power that we cannot understand.

The men who wrote the **Gospels** wanted to show why they believed that Jesus was special. They included the stories about the miracles which Jesus had done to show why they believed that Jesus had special power. Christians believe that this power came from God.

There are 35 stories about miracles in the Gospels. In some of the stories, Jesus made very ill people better. In others, he made "impossible" things happen. Christians believe that he could do these things because he was God's Son.

Calming the storm

You can find this story in the Bible in Mark's Gospel, chapter 4 verses 35–41.

Many of Jesus's friends were fishermen. They had boats on the Sea of Galilee. One night, Jesus was with some of his disciples in a boat on the sea. He was tired and had gone to sleep. Suddenly a storm blew up. The **disciples** were frightened and thought they were going to die. They woke Jesus up. They asked if he did not care that they were in danger.

Jesus stood up in the boat. He told the wind to stop blowing, and the waves to be calm. The storm stopped. The disciples did not understand what had happened, but it made them more sure that Jesus was special.

The Sea of Galilee today. Many of Jesus's miracles happened in this area.

An old picture made of tiles showing the loaves and fish

Jesus feeds 5,000 people

You can find this story in the Bible in John's Gospel, chapter 6 verses 1–14.

Jesus had been teaching a crowd of people all day. It was getting late and the disciples said he should send the people home. Instead, Jesus told the disciples to find food for them.

They found a boy who had a packed lunch with him. He had five bread rolls and two small fish. The disciples did not think this would be any use, but Jesus took the food and said a prayer, asking God to bless it. Then he told the disciples to hand out the food to the crowd. Everyone had enough to eat, and there was enough left over to fill 12 food baskets.

A modern hymn

This is part of a **hymn** which shows how Christians believe God's power still works today.

Father, I place into your hands
The things that I can't do.
Father, I place into your hands
The times that I've been through.
Father, I place into your hands
The way that I should go,
For I know I always can trust you.

Father, I place into your hands
My friends and family.
Father, I place into your hands
The things that trouble me.
Father, I place into your hands
The person I would be,
For I know I always can trust you.

Father, we love to seek your face
We love to hear your voice.
Father, we love to sing your praise
And in your name rejoice.
Father, we love to walk with you
And in your presence rest,
For we know we always can trust you.

How Christianity grew

This section tells you about the early years of Christianity.

The beginning of a new religion
Jesus and all his first **disciples** were Jews. They did not want to start a new religion. People who followed Jesus's teachings were just Jews who believed that Jesus was special. Then, little by little, problems began.

Early problems
In those days, Jews tried to have nothing to do with people who were not Jews. They would not eat with anyone who was not Jewish. They would not go into the house of anyone who was not Jewish. They tried not to talk to anyone who was not Jewish.

People who were not Jews heard about Jesus. They wanted to follow his teachings, too. At first, this caused many problems. There were arguments and discussions about it. Could it be allowed? At last, it was decided that people who were not Jews could still become followers of Jesus. This was very important. It meant that the new religion could reach far more people.

St Paul
One man was especially important helping Christianity to spread. He was a Jew called Saul. At first, Saul was very angry when he heard what the Christians were teaching. He thought it was wrong to **worship** a man like they worshipped Jesus.

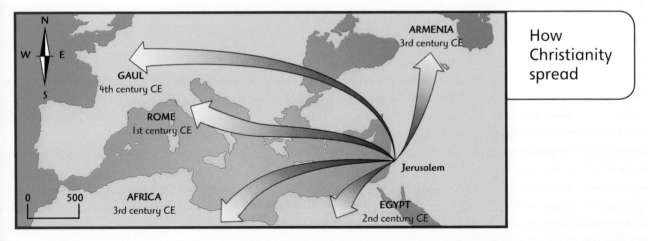

How Christianity spread

This early Christian statue shows Jesus as the Good Shepherd.

Saul went to see the leaders of the Jews. He explained how he felt, and they agreed with him. They gave Saul permission to arrest as many Christians as he could find. He set off to a town called Damascus. He knew that some Christians were there. On the way something amazing happened to him. He had a **vision**. He was told by Jesus to stop punishing the Christians. After this, Saul became a Christian and changed his name to Paul.

He spent the rest of his life travelling and teaching people about Christianity. His life was very hard, but he said it was worth it to be able to preach about Jesus. Paul was an important Christian teacher.

St Paul's teachings

Many of the letters which St Paul wrote to his Christian friends are in the Bible. These are some of the things he said.

Be kind and loving to each other. Forgive each other. (Ephesians 4: 32)

If someone does wrong to you, don't pay him back by doing wrong to him. (Romans 12: 17)

Don't worry about things. Pray and ask God for everything you need. (Philippians 4: 6)

Love is patient and kind. Love is not ill-mannered or selfish. Love never gives up. (I Corinthians 13: 4–7)

Be brave, be strong. Do all your work in love. (I Corinthians 16: 13–14)

The saints

This section tells you about some Christian saints.

What is a saint?
A **saint** is someone who lived an especially good life. Saints were very close to God when they were alive.

Christians believe that because they were so good when they were alive, saints are still special after their death. Many Christians pray to saints, because they think that the saints can help them.

Many of Jesus's **disciples** are called saints. Two of the most popular are St Peter and St Andrew. They were both **crucified** because they were Christians. (Notice that Saint is often written as "St".)

An old painting showing St Andrew

Patron saints
Some saints are thought to have special interests. This may be because of where the saint lived when he or she was alive, or because of the job they did. They are called **patron saints**. (A patron is someone who looks after people.)

St Nicholas
St Nicholas is the patron saint of children. Nicholas lived in the country that we call Turkey. He was a kind man who helped young people. After he died, it became the custom to give children presents on his special day, 6 December. In some countries, children are still given presents on this day. In time, this custom became mixed up with Christmas, because of the idea that Jesus was a gift from God to the world. So St Nicholas became known as Santa Claus.

St Francis

St Francis was born in the town of Assisi in Italy in 1181 CE. His father was a rich shop-keeper, and Francis could have had an easy life. But he felt that God was telling him to live in a different way. He gave up all his belongings and spent his life caring for people who were poor.

Pilgrimage

Many people think that the place where a saint lived or died is important. Sometimes they go on a special journey to visit it. This journey is called a **pilgrimage**. One of the most important places of pilgrimage in Britain is Canterbury **Cathedral**. This is where St Thomas Becket was killed in 1170 CE.

Patron saints

Many areas of life have a patron saint. The patron saint of love is St Valentine. People send cards to people they love on 14 February, which is St Valentine's Day. The patron saint of travellers is St Christopher. An old story says he was a giant who carried the child Jesus across a river. Years ago, people believed that if they saw a picture of St Christopher, they would not die that day.

St Polycarp was a Christian who lived in Turkey many years ago. He said he would rather shut his ears than listen to people who were not telling the truth, so he has become the patron saint of people with earache!

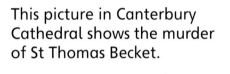

This picture in Canterbury Cathedral shows the murder of St Thomas Becket.

Christianity today

This section tells you something about being a Christian today.

Christianity is the largest religion in the world. Different Christians live in different ways. Not all of them believe exactly the same things. Some Christians think that it is enough just to believe in Jesus. Other Christians believe they should give their whole life to God.

Monks and nuns

Monks and **nuns** are ordinary men and women. They have decided to live their lives in a special way. They want to spend their whole life serving God and helping other people. Some monks and nuns help others by working with people, for example as teachers or nurses.

Some spend their time praying for other people.

All monks and nuns make special promises, which are called **vows**. For example, they promise not to marry. This means they can think about their work, and they do not have to care for a family.

They promise they will not own things. They are given things they need, such as clothes and food. This means they do not have to worry about money and possessions.

They promise they will follow the rules of their group. This means they do not have to think about the way they live. All these things mean they are free to think about God.

Nuns and monks work in many different ways.

Drink a **fair** cup of coffee!

These friends drink Cafédirect happily, knowing the pickers of this coffee have decent conditions. It is the first fairly traded supermarket coffee.

Christian Aid

A Christian Aid poster

Helping others

Christians believe that helping other people is important. They believe that God cares about everyone in the world. Christians should care about people, too.

Some Christians spend all their time working with people who need help. Some spend their spare time helping other people. Some Christians give money so that other people can be helped. All Christians try to live in a way that does not harm others.

Christian Aid

The picture of a poster on this page is about the work of Christian Aid. "Aid" is another word for help. Christian Aid is the name of a group which tries to make life better for people who live in very poor countries of the world. It is run by people who are Christians, but it does not just help Christians.

Christian Aid collects money from people in rich countries like Britain, and uses it to help the poorest people, no matter who they are. Sometimes the money is used for things like food and blankets when there is an emergency. Other money is used for things like teaching, so that people can learn to help themselves. Christians believe that caring about other people is important, because it is what Jesus taught.

Christmas

This section tells you about Christmas time.

Advent

Advent means "coming". It is the name given to the four weeks before Christmas. At Christmas, Christians remember Jesus's birth. So Advent is the time when Christians look forward to Christmas, the time when Jesus came to earth.

In Advent, Christians use special candles and calendars. Advent candles have little marks to show the days until Christmas. The candle is lit each day and burns down to the next mark.

There are also Advent calendars. They have little doors to open, one for each day. Behind each door is a picture. Candles and calendars like this help to remind people that Christmas is coming closer. They also remind people how important Christmas is.

Christmas

No one knows the exact date when Jesus was born. In those days, people did not keep careful records. When Christians began to celebrate it, they chose a date that was already special. This is why, in most parts of the world, Christmas Day is on 25 December. (In countries where Orthodox Christians live, the date is 6 January.)

Christmas is the time when Christians remember the birth of Jesus. They believe that this was very important, because Jesus was God's Son.

Christians usually try to go to church at Christmas. There are often special **services**. One of the most important services

An Advent calendar and candle

A Christmas crib, which shows how people imagine the birth of Jesus in Bethlehem

is called Midnight Mass. It is held at midnight on Christmas Eve.

The services include Bible readings about Jesus's birth and special songs called **carols**. Christians thank God for giving his son Jesus to the world. Christmas is now also a holiday for many people who are not Christians.

Boxing Day

Boxing Day is 26 December. Hundreds of years ago, people put money in special boxes which were kept in churches. On Boxing Day the boxes were opened and the money was given to the poor.

Why 25 December?

25 December was special because it was the shortest day of the year. On that day people **worshipped** the sun and prayed it would come back and give them another summer. It was a holiday when people gave each other presents and had a good time.

For Christians who believed that God made everything including the sun it was an easy step to remember the Son of God on this day. Today, the calendar is different and the shortest day of the year is 21 December, but the birth of Jesus is still celebrated on 25 December.

Easter

This section tells you about the most important time of year for Christians.

Lent

Lent is the name for the six weeks before Easter. It is a very serious time of year for Christians. They remember the time when Jesus was in the desert thinking about how to do the work God wanted. Christians try to live especially good lives during Lent. The day before Lent begins is called Shrove Tuesday.

Shrove Tuesday

Shrove is a very old word. It means being forgiven for things you have done wrong. For some Christians, it is an important day for going to **confession** (see page 11). Shrove Tuesday is a time for a new start before Lent. Another name for Shrove Tuesday is Pancake Day. Many years ago, people used to eat very plain foods in Lent. It became the custom to eat pancakes which are made of fat and eggs on Shrove Tuesday, to use up these rich foods before Lent began.

Ash Wednesday

On Ash Wednesday some Christians go to a very serious **church service**. Special ash is put on their forehead in the shape of a cross. It is a sign that they are really sorry for all the things that they have done wrong.

Easter

Easter is the most important Christian festival. It takes place in spring, and it is a festival of new life. Christians remember Jesus's death and his coming back to life, which is called the **Resurrection**.

Easter eggs are a symbol of new life.

An Orthodox
service at Easter

Good Friday

On Good Friday, Christians remember that Jesus was **crucified**. Christians believe that this opened up a way to God.

That is why it is called Good Friday, even though Jesus died. It is a sad day. Churches never have flowers on Good Friday.

Easter Sunday

Easter Sunday is a joyful day. Christians believe that Jesus rose from the dead on this day. They believe that this changed the world for ever. Many Christians make a particular effort to go to church on Easter Day, because it is so important.

Easter eggs

Long before Jesus's time, eggs were thought to be special. They do not seem to be alive, but contain life inside them. After the Resurrection of Jesus, it was an easy step for Christians to think of eggs as a sign of new life. Eggs have always been part of Easter celebrations.

Long ago, carved eggs made of wood or precious stones were given as gifts. When people first had the idea of making eggs to eat, they were made of marzipan or sugar. In the last 200 years, chocolate eggs have become popular.

Other celebrations

This section tells you about two other Christian celebrations.

Pentecost

Pentecost takes place 50 days after Easter. At Pentecost, Christians think about something that is hard to understand, but important.

They remember when the first Christians were given the **Holy Spirit**. Christians believe the Holy Spirit is God's power. It is the way God works through people. At Pentecost, the first Christians were given this power. They could teach people and make ill people well.

They could do the things that Jesus did. Because this was so important, many people say that Pentecost is like the birthday of Christianity. It was the day that Christianity began.

At Pentecost, many Christians join in walks around their town or village. They want to show what they believe and that they are Christians. They believe the Holy Spirit is still working today and helps them to live better lives.

The other name for Pentecost is Whit Sunday. This goes back to the days when people often joined the **Church** and were **baptized** on this day. They wore white clothes, and so the day was called White (Whit) Sunday.

Harvest festival

Harvest festivals are usually held in September or October. They are a time for saying "thank you". Christians believe that God made everything in the world, so at harvest time they thank him for providing food and all the other things that we need to live.

Many Christians join in processions at Pentecost.

44

Hundreds of years ago, most people were farmers. Harvest festivals were a time when they had finished the harvest. They could thank God that the crops had been safely harvested.

Today, most people are not farmers. But people can still thank God for food and for the people who work to provide food. Harvest festivals remind people that everyone must work together.

Special church services are held for harvest festivals. Churches are decorated with lots of fruit and flowers. Often, there are also things like bread and water because they are necessary for life. They remind people to thank God for everything.

Churches are decorated for harvest festival.

A prayer for harvest
This harvest prayer was written by a nine-year-old girl.

Thank you Jesus
For the fishermen who work all day.
Thank you for the farmers
Who grow wheat for our cereals
And corn for our flour and bread.
For the vineyard owners
Who grow grapes for our wine.
Thank you for our milk and cream;
*   and for our cheese and lollies;*
Thank you for our apples, lemons,
Oranges, pears, and our potatoes
And beans, carrots,
And lots of other vegetables;
For our salads like peppers,
*   tomatoes, and cucumbers.*
But most of all, thank you
For the rain and the sun,
That make the harvest grow
*   for everyone.*

Baptism and confirmation

This section tells you about special services that are held when people join the Church.

Baptism

Baptism is a service when someone joins the **Church**. In most Churches, the person being baptized is a baby. The baby's parents promise that they will bring the child up to believe in Jesus.

Baptizing a baby

Baptism is often part of an ordinary **church service**. The parents and friends of the baby's family stand near the font. The font is a special basin which contains **holy** water. The **vicar** or **priest** uses a little of the water to make the shape of a cross on the baby's forehead.

As they do this, they say the baby's name. For example, imagine the parents had chosen the names Thomas Joseph. The vicar would say "I baptize you Thomas Joseph in the name of the Father, and of the Son, and of the **Holy Spirit**."

A baptism in the Baptist Church

In the Baptist Church, babies are not baptized. Baptists think that someone being baptized should be old enough to make promises for themselves. When they baptize people, they do not use a font. The person being baptized walks down some steps into a special tank of water in the floor of the church. They promise they are sorry for things they have done wrong.

People

They promise that they believe in Jesus; Then their whole body is carefully tipped under the water. They usually leave the pool by a different set of steps. This is to show they are starting a new life with Jesus.

In the Orthodox Church, babies are baptized with water by being put right into the font. Then they have special oil put on eight places on their body. This is called **Chrismation**.

Confirmation

Confirmation is a service held by Churches which baptize babies. To confirm something means saying it is really true.

The Confirmation service is to let people make for themselves the promises that were made for them when they were babies.

In the Anglican and Roman Catholic Churches, Confirmation is usually carried out by a bishop. In other Churches, it is carried out by the person who leads services. Each person who is going to be confirmed answers questions about what they believe, and the bishop lays his hands on their head as he prays for them. After the service, the person is counted as a full member of their Church.

A Confirmation prayer

This prayer could be used by people who are being confirmed.

*Father God, I thank you that
    now I can make for myself the
    promises which were made
    for me by others when I was
    baptized.
May your Holy Spirit confirm
    and strengthen my faith.
May I grow to take a fuller part
    in the life of the Church.
May your Holy Spirit help me
    to live so that I can follow the
    teachings of Jesus.
I ask these things in the name
    of Jesus.
Amen.*

Marriage and death

This section tells you what Christians believe about marriage and death.

Marriage

Christians believe that God wants men and women to marry so that they can help each other. Many Christians choose to marry in **church**, but they do not have to.

Some of the words of the marriage **service** must be included by law, because the service has to obey the law of the country. As well as the couple and the **vicar**, at least two other people must be present, as witnesses.

The people who are getting married are called the bride and bridegroom. In the marriage service, they say that they do not know any reason why they should not marry each other. Then they promise that they will love each other and stay together until one of them dies. They usually give each other a ring. There are prayers asking God to look after them in their life together.

The service ends with the bride and bridegroom signing their names in a special book. This is called the register. The law says that the register must be signed.

Divorce

Sometimes a couple do not stay married until one of them dies. If a marriage is ended while the husband and wife are still alive, it is called a **divorce**.

Some Christians believe that divorce is wrong. Others believe that a divorced man or woman should be able to marry someone else if they want to. Some Churches do not allow people to marry again in church if they have been divorced.

The bride and groom exchange wedding rings.

A funeral service in a Roman Catholic church

Death

When someone dies, there is a special service called a funeral. A funeral includes prayers for the person who has died, and for their family and friends. **Hymns** are sung, and there is usually a talk about the person and the things that made him or her special.

Christians believe that death is not the end of a person. Belief that there is life after death is an important part of Christian teaching. Christians believe that the body is left behind, and a person's **soul** begins a new life with God. So for Christians a funeral is a time of hope as well.

Signs used in a wedding service

While they are making their promises to each other, the bride and bridegroom hold hands as if they are shaking hands. This goes back to the days when shaking hands after you had agreed something was a sign that you would not go back on your word. The rings that a couple give each other are a sign of the promises that they have made.

In Orthodox wedding services, the bride and bridegroom are given crowns to wear by the priest. They are made of leaves and flowers or gold and silver. They are a sign that God will look after them in their marriage.

Glossary

altar special table used in churches

Amen word used in prayers to show agreement

angel messenger from God

baptism special service when people join the Church

bishop senior vicar

carol joyful song

cathedral important and large church

Chrismation service held in Orthodox churches in which oil is put on a baby

Christ God's chosen one

church 1. building where Christians meet to worship, 2. a group or community of Christians

confession saying what you have done wrong

Confirmation service in which people make baptism promises again, for themselves

crucify kill by nailing to a cross

disciples special friends of Jesus

divorce the ending of a marriage

Eucharist "thanksgiving", service where Christians remember the death and resurrection of Jesus Christ, using bread and wine

Gospel part of the New Testament which tells of the life of Jesus

governor ruler, person in charge

Holy Communion most important Christian service, also called the Eucharist

holy to do with God

hymn special song used in worship

icon picture used in worship, showing Jesus, Mary or one of the saints

Judaism religion of the Jews

Lord's Prayer prayer which Christians believe Jesus taught to his friends

meeting word used by the Society of Friends instead of service

miracle something that happens that seems impossible and shows special power

monk man who belongs to a special religious group

nun woman who belongs to a special religious group

parable story with a special meaning

parish local area with its own church, which might be a village or part of a town

patron saint saint who has a special interest in a country, job or situation

pilgrimage journey that someone makes to visit a place which is important in their religion

Pope head of the Roman Catholic Church

priest someone set apart to lead worship

Resurrection Jesus's coming back to life

saint someone very close to God

service meeting to worship God

soul spirit that is inside each of us

spire pointed part of a church roof

spirit a being who is alive but does not have a body

Testament one of the two parts of the Bible

vicar Anglican priest

vision special sort of dream, especially one to do with religion

vow very serious promise, usually one that is expected to last for life

worship to show respect and love for God

Find out more

More books to read

Barnes, Trevor. *World Faiths: Christianity*. London, Kingfisher, 2005

Nason, Ruth. *Religious Lives: Jesus and Christianity*, London, Hodder Wayland, 2006

Penney, Sue. *World beliefs and cultures: Christianity*. Oxford, Heinemann Library, 2001

Using the internet

You can find out more about Christianity in books and on the Internet. Use a search engine such as **www.yahooligans.com** to search for information. A search for the word "Christianity" will bring back lots of results, but it may be difficult to find the information you want. Try refining your search to look for some of the people and ideas mentioned in this book, such as "St Francis" or "Christian worship".

Website

www.bbc.co.uk/religion/religions/christianity/index
Try looking here for up-to-date information and articles on Christianity and Christians.

Index

The numbers in **bold** tell you where you can find out most about the words.